EXPRESSING OUR LOVE

EXPRESSING OUR LOVE

Wedding poems for today's couples

Including a section
on personalizing
your own wedding ceremony

Edited by Susan Polis Schutz
Illustrated by SandPiper Studios

Blue Mountain Press ™

Boulder, Colorado

Library of Congress Number: 78-75371
ISBN: 0-88396-042-7

Manufactured in the United States of America
First Printing: March, 1979

Blue Mountain Press INC

P.O. Box 4549, Boulder, Colorado 80306

ACKNOWLEDGMENTS:
Thanks to the SandPiper Studios staff, including Cliff Scott and Jim Turrentine, with special thanks to Faith Hamilton and Douglas Pagels.

We gratefully acknowledge the permission granted by the following authors, songwriters, publishers and authors' representatives to reprint poems and excerpts from their publications.

Owepar Publishing Co. for "With open-minded understanding," by Dolly Parton. From the song BETWEEN US. Copyright © 1972 by Owepar Publishing Co. And for "I have come to know," by Dolly Parton. From the song HOW DOES IT FEEL TO KNOW. Copyright © 1976 by Owepar Publishing Co. All rights reserved. Reprinted by permission.

Leonard Nimoy for "Whatever we are," "You are the dream" and "There is no peace," by Leonard Nimoy. From the book COME BE WITH ME. Copyright © Leonard Nimoy, 1978. And for "Thank you for a world," by Leonard Nimoy. From the book WE ARE ALL CHILDREN SEARCHING FOR LOVE. Copyright © Leonard Nimoy, 1977. All rights reserved. Reprinted by permission.

Harcourt Brace Jovanovich, Inc. for "if everything happens," by E.E. Cummings. Copyright 1944 by E.E. Cummings; renewed 1972 by Nancy T. Andrews. Reprinted from COMPLETE POEMS 1913-1962 by E.E. Cummings by permission of Harcourt Brace Jovanovich, Inc. All rights reserved.

Celestial Arts for "Love me," by Walter Rinder. From the book THE HUMANNESS OF YOU VOL. I. Copyright © 1973 by Walter Rinder. All rights reserved. Reprinted by permission.

Lady Jane Music for "Come stand by my side," by Hoyt Axton. From the song LESS THAN THE SONG. Copyright © 1972 by Lady Jane Music. And for "Holy is the taking," by Hoyt Axton. From the song AIR MAIL. Copyright © 1971, 1972 by Lady Jane Music. And for "You are the object," by Hoyt Axton. From the song GYPSY MOTH. Copyright © 1976 by Lady Jane Music. And for "I am the sea," by Hoyt Axton. From the song EPISTLE. Copyright © 1968, 1972 by Lady Jane Music. All rights reserved. Reprinted by permission.

Diane Westlake for "new love soars," by Diane Westlake. From the book GENTLE FREEDOM. Copyright © 1977 Diane Westlake. And for "Prayer," by Diane Westlake. Copyright © 1978 Diane Westlake. All rights reserved. Reprinted by permission.

Macmillan Publishing Co., Inc. for "Love is all force," by Woody Guthrie. From the book BORN TO WIN, edited by Robert Shelton. Copyright © The Guthrie Children's Trust Fund 1965. All rights reserved. Reprinted by permission.

Jack V. Crawford for "A Marriage Covenant," by Jack V. Crawford. Copyright © Jack V. Crawford, 1976. All rights reserved. Reprinted by permission.

Harold Ober Associates for "My deepest, strongest desire," by Woodrow Wilson. And for "I would that I could," by Ellen Wilson. From the book THE PRICELESS GIFT, published by Alfred A. Knopf, Inc. Copyright © 1962 by Eleanor Wilson McAdoo. All rights reserved. Reprinted by permission.

Alfred A. Knopf, Inc. for "Among intelligent people," by Kahlil Gibran. And for "Nothing you become," by Mary Haskell. From the book BELOVED PROPHET: The Love Letters of Kahlil Gibran and Mary Haskell, and Her Private Journal, by Kahlil Gibran and Mary Haskell, edited and arranged by Virginia Hilu. Copyright © 1972 by Alfred A. Knopf, Inc. And for "On Marriage," by Kahlil Gibran. From the book THE PROPHET. Copyright 1923 by Kahlil Gibran; renewal Copyright 1951 by Administrators C.T.A. of Kahlil Gibran Estate, and Mary G. Gibran. All rights reserved. Reprinted by permission of Alfred A. Knopf, Inc.

Alfred A. Knopf, Inc. for "You will never know," by Isadora Duncan. From the book YOUR ISADORA: THE LOVE STORY OF ISADORA DUNCAN AND GORDON CRAIG TOLD THROUGH LETTERS AND DIARIES, by Francis Steegmuller. Copyright © 1974 by Francis Steegmuller. Copyright © 1974 by The New York Public Library. Reprinted by permission of Random House, Inc. All rights reserved.

Lanny Allen for "Wedding Pledge," by Lanny Allen. Copyright © 1978 by Lanny Allen. All rights reserved. Reprinted by permission.

Doubleday & Company, Inc. for "Marriage isn't mutual ownership," by Hugh Prather. From the book NOTES ON LOVE AND COURAGE. Copyright © 1977 by Hugh Prather. All rights reserved. Reprinted by permission.

The Citadel Press for "Of Marriage," by Kahlil Gibran. From the book A SECOND TREASURY OF KAHLIL GIBRAN, translated by Anthony R. Ferris. Copyright © 1962 by The Citadel Press. All rights reserved. Reprinted by permission.

Harper & Row Publishers, Inc. for "A good marriage," by Pearl S. Buck. From p. 54 of TO MY DAUGHTERS WITH LOVE, by Pearl S. Buck (John Day). Copyright 1949 © 1957, 1960, 1962, 1963, 1964 by Pearl S. Buck. Copyright © 1967 by the Pearl S. Buck Foundation, Inc. Reprinted by permission of Harper & Row Publishers, Inc. All rights reserved.

Continental Publications for "Your heart is my heart," by Susan Polis Schutz. Copyright © Continental Publications, 1971. And for "Because our relationship," by Susan Polis Schutz. Copyright © Continental Publications, 1975. And for "I'm not that kind of girl." And for "I do not want to change you," "Though we are very close" and "One of the important aspects," by Susan Polis Schutz. Copyright © Continental Publications, 1976. From the book YOURS IF YOU ASK. And for "We all need," "Thinking of home," "Today I realized" and "Each dawn," by Louise Bradford Lowell. Copyright © Continental Publications, 1978. All rights reserved. Reprinted by permission.

A careful effort has been made to trace the ownership of poems used in this anthology in order to obtain permission to reprint copyrighted material and to give proper credit to the copyright owners.

If any error or omission has occurred, it is completely inadvertent, and we would like to make corrections in future editions provided that written notification is made to the publisher: BLUE MOUNTAIN PRESS, INC., P.O. Box 4549, Boulder, Colorado 80306

CONTENTS

Introduction

The seeds of a relationship are planted magically, miraculously—and left to grow in the light and warmth of two people in love. As the roots of a relationship intertwine, they go out in search of strength and security. Growing with the passing of time, these roots are nourished by trust, faith and the recognition of a mutual goal . . . a desire to always be together.

It is often at this point of realization in a relationship that marriage is discussed. Marriage is the natural extension of enduring love. It continues to be one of the most time-honored institutions of civilization.

Many individuals will find their wedding date to be the most important time in their lives . . . a time when celebration and ceremony combine to symbolize a natural unity and a new beginning. Rich in history, custom and tradition, the wedding ceremony of today bears a striking resemblance to the vows and services of long ago. Many contemporary couples object to the idea of a "carbon copy" wedding. And for good reason. They would prefer to take part in a ceremony that is relevant and expressive of their own lives.

Expressing Our Love offers information on how to personalize your wedding by writing your own wedding vows and creating your own ceremony. By orienting a wedding service toward yourselves—as individuals—you are certain to have a unique and unforgettable ceremony.

We have started this book with a large section of poetry and prose selections, including quotes from the Bible and American Indian prayers, and ranging from Shakespeare and Mark Twain to Susan Polis Schutz, Leonard Nimoy and Kahlil Gibran. Many of these selections, in addition to being our favorites, have actually been used in weddings, and they should help to facilitate your search for personal and meaningful expressions of your love.

The closing sections of the book are concerned with traditional vows, creativity in writing vows, group participation, poetry and musical selections, invitations, guests, settings and symbols. The book furnishes guidelines for taking your service from a "rough draft" to a final version. We have included a complete unique wedding ceremony in the closing chapter to serve as an example of a personalized wedding.

A wedding should create a mood and a feeling that will be as magical as your love for each other, and it should capture the beauty of a moment that will reflect your personalities, your life-styles, your beliefs and your dreams. We hope that Expressing Our Love helps you to achieve this.

With our blessings to the wedding couple, express your love . . . and enjoy it to the fullest.

Wedding poems and prose selections

I do not
want to change you
You know what
is best for you
much better than I

I do not
want you to change me
I want you to
accept me and respect me
the way I am

In this way
we can build
a strong relationship
based on reality
rather than a dream

—Susan Polis Schutz

Though we are very close
to each other,
we each have our
own lives and own goals.
We are together, always,
in our hearts,
but not necessarily
        together, always,
in all our activities—
a relationship
based on
truth and freedom.

—Susan Polis Schutz

Of Marriage

Marriage is the union of two souls in a strong love for the abolishment of separateness. It is that higher unity which fuses the separate unities within the two spirits. It is the golden ring in a chain whose beginning is a glance, and whose ending is Eternity. It is the pure rain that falls from an unblemished sky to fructify and bless the fields of divine Nature.

As the first glance from the eyes of the beloved is like a seed sown in the human heart, and the first kiss of her lips like a flower upon the branch of the Tree of Life, so the union of two lovers in marriage is like the first fruit of the first flower of that seed.

—Kahlil Gibran

Whatever we are
  We belong together

Wherever we are
  We will find each other

Whoever we are
  We are
    Forever one

—Leonard Nimoy

A marriage . . .
makes of two fractional lives
 a whole;
it gives to two purposeless lives
a work, and doubles the strength
of each to perform it;
it gives to two
questioning natures
a reason for living,
and something to live for;
it will give a new gladness
to the sunshine,
a new fragrance to the flowers,
a new beauty to the earth,
and a new mystery to life.

—Mark Twain

The most wonderful
of all things in life,
I believe, is the discovery
of another human being
with whom one's relationship
has a glowing depth, beauty,
and joy as the years increase.
This inner progressiveness
of love between
two human beings
is a most marvelous thing,
it cannot be found
by looking for it or
by passionately wishing for it.
It is a sort of Divine accident.

—Sir Hugh Walpole

I give you my hand!
I give you my love more precious than money,
I give you myself before preaching or law;
Will you give me yourself? will you come travel with me?
Shall we stick by each other as long as we live?

—Walt Whitman

You will never know how beautiful you are. Only I
know that. You will never know what an immense
Joy Giver you are. All that joy is with me. You have
given joy & love unspeakable. What shall I give you
in return—All, all that I have in my power to give . . .

You have the most beautiful eyes in the world—&
the dearest hands. You contain the sweetness of all
the flowers & soft winds & sun—& I love you—

—Isadora Duncan

You have brought me peace;
The peace of great tranquil waters,
and the quiet of the summer sea.
Your hands are filled with peace
as the noon-tide is filled with light;
about your head is bound
the eternal quiet of the stars,
and in your heart dwells
the calm miracle of twilight.
I am utterly content.
In all my spirit is no ripple of unrest,
For I have opened unto you
the wide gates of my being
And like a tide
you have flowed into me.

—Eunice Tietjens

Wedding Pledge

Summer's warm breeze
  Is beckoning a new life

Now our thoughts will rendezvous
  Into a beautiful dream

As you take my hand
  A soft strength overwhelms me

To know that I'm loved
  For this day we pledge

Ourselves in love . . . forever.

—Lanny Allen

Love is eternal.
The aspect may change,
but not the essence.

—Vincent Van Gogh

love me because I try to touch life
          within the framework of uncertainty
love me in the shadows of my indecisions
          as I strive to gain knowledge
love me in the silence of my hurts
          and the noise of my confusions
love me for the feeling of my heart
          not the fears of my mind
love me in my search for truth
          though I may stumble upon fallacy
love me as I pursue my dreams
          sometimes retarded by illusions
love me as I grow to know myself
          even during the times of stagnation
love me because I seek God's harmony
          not man's discord
love me for my body that I wish to share
          with affection, wrapping you in warmth
love me because we are different
          as we are the same
love me that our time together will be spent
          in growing, kindling the world
          with understanding
love me not with expectations
          but with hope
I will love you the same.

                              —Walter Rinder

My deepest, strongest desire in marrying you, darling, is to make you happy, and I would put into this some word of love which would seem to your heart a sort of sweet preface to the book of love which we are about to open together, to read new secrets of sympathy and companionship. I would have you catch a glimpse of my purpose for the future and of the joy which that future contains for me, of the gratitude I feel for your priceless gift of love, and of the infinite love and tenderness which is the gift of my whole heart to you.

—Woodrow Wilson

I would that I could tell you something more than I have ever told before of what love means for me. But there are few places in my heart which I have not opened to you, dearest; I have shown you my heart of hearts. I know because your own words tell me that you have read it and read it aright. You know as well as you can know, before the years have brought their proof, how absolutely I am yours; you know the depth and tenderness and fervour of my love —this "all-controlling love"; you know how absolutely I believe in you, with what unquestioning confidence. And I believe that you trust me as my love deserves, that you will rest in my love ever as I in yours.

—Ellen Wilson

love you
not as something private
and personal,
   which is my own,
but as something universal
and worthy of love
which I have found.

—Henry David Thoreau

oming
      together
   is a beginning;
      Keeping
         together
      is progress;
Working
      together
      is success.

—Anonymous

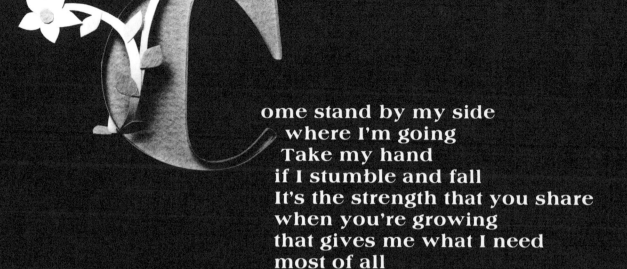

ome stand by my side
  where I'm going
   Take my hand
if I stumble and fall
It's the strength that you share
when you're growing
that gives me what I need
most of all

—Hoyt Axton

ove consists in this;
that two solitudes protect
and touch and greet
each other.

—Rainer Maria Rilke

I love you
not only for what you are
but for what I am
when I am with you.

I love you
not only for what
you have made of yourself
but for what
you are making of me.

I love you
for the part of me
that you bring out;
I love you
for putting your hand
into my heaped-up heart
and passing over
all the foolish, weak things
that you can't help
dimly seeing there,
and for drawing out
into the light
all the beautiful belongings
that no one else had looked
quite far enough to find.

I love you because you
are helping me to make
of the lumber of my life
not a tavern
but a temple;

out of works
of my every day
not a reproach
but a song.

I love you
because you have done
more than any creed
could have done
to make me good,
and more than any fate
could have done
to make me happy.

You have done it
without a touch,
without a word,
without a sign.
You have done it
by being yourself.
Perhaps that is what
being a friend means,
after all.

—Roy Croft

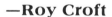

To Husband and Wife

Preserve sacredly
the privacies of your home,
your married state
and your heart.

With mutual help
build your quiet world.
Let moments of alienation,
if they occur, be healed at once.
To each other confess
and all will come out right.
Never let the morrow's sun
still find you at variance.
Renew and renew your vow.
It will do you good;
and thereby your minds
will grow together
contented in that love
which is stronger than death,
and you will be truly one.

—Margaret Springdale

You are the dream
    I dream

You are the sun
    I seek

You are
    My shade

You are the rest
    I sleep

    You are the peace
      I yearn for

    You are
      My hope,
        My love

      —Leonard Nimoy

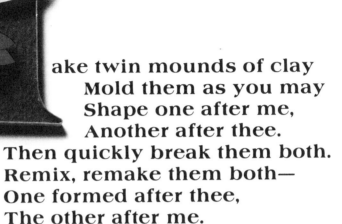

ake twin mounds of clay
        Mold them as you may
        Shape one after me,
        Another after thee.
Then quickly break them both.
Remix, remake them both—
One formed after thee,
The other after me.

Part of my clay is thine;
Part of thy clay is mine.

                    —Kwan Tao-Shing

new love soars bringing courage and light hearted joy
everything is possible . . . each moment apart is emptiness
the world looks like your lover . . . desire consumes
togetherness brings the truth that two are one
each one's thought is as the other's simultaneous discovery
wholeness of person replaces life's incompleteness
time passes and feelings settle to comfortable security
understanding the need to give time and patience
always a bit of yourself . . . compromise
with no loss of identity . . . both of you
giving and taking rising above insignificant faults
the thread of love weaves life's patterns everchanging
each of you grows and moves in new directions
giving tender care to your times together
unique individuals sharing what you are
two special beings . . . you are eachother

—Diane Westlake

Love is all force.
Love is all power.
Love is all energy.
Love is all strength.
Love is all health.
Love is all beauty.
Love is all good work well done.
Love is all fun.
Love is all pleasure, all joys known.
Love is all eternity.
Love is here now.

—Woody Guthrie

How do I love thee? Let me count the ways.
I love thee to the depth and breadth and height
My soul can reach, when feeling out of sight
For the ends of Being and ideal Grace.
I love thee to the level of everyday's
Most quiet need, by sun and candle-light.
I love thee freely, as men strive for Right;
I love thee purely, as they turn from Praise.
I love thee with the passion put to use
In my old griefs, and with my childhood's faith.
I love thee with a love I seemed to lose
With my lost saints, — I love thee with the breath,
Smiles, tears, of all my life! — and, if God choose,
I shall but love thee better after death.

—Elizabeth Barrett Browning

We all need
a person to understand
Someone to share our
thoughts with
and always be around
in time of need
We all need
a person like you

—Louise Bradford Lowell

Thinking of home
Thinking of the past
Thinking of tomorrow
Brings me closer to you
You are a special person
who brings lasting joy
into my life

—Louise Bradford Lowell

You give me space
to belong to myself
yet without separating me
from your own life.
May it all turn out
to your happiness.

—Johann Wolfgang von Goethe

Today I realized
how much I need you
I love to spend
time with you
I can discuss my feelings
with you honestly
I can share things
with you

—Louise Bradford Lowell

Come live with me
  and be my Love,
And we will
  all the pleasures prove
That hills and valleys,
  dales and fields,
Or woods
  or steepy mountain yields.

The shepherd swains
  shall dance and sing
For thy delight
  each May morning;
If these delights
  thy mind may move,
Come live with me
  and be my Love.

—Christopher Marlowe

Nothing you become
will disappoint me;
I have no preconception
that I'd like to see you be or do.
I have no desire
to foresee you,
only to discover you.
You can't disappoint me.

—Mary Haskell

Among intelligent people
the surest basis for marriage
is friendship—
the sharing of real interests—
the ability to fight out
ideas together
and understand each other's
thoughts
and dreams.

—Kahlil Gibran

y beloved spake, and said unto me,
Rise up, my love, my fair one,
and come away.
For, lo, the winter is past,
The rain is over and gone;
The flowers appear on the earth;
The time of the singing of birds is come,
And the voice of the turtle is heard in our land;
The fig tree putteth forth her green figs,
And the vines with the tender grape
Give a good smell.
Arise, my love, my fair one, and come away.

—The Song of Solomon 2:10-13

. . . a man leaves his father
and mother, and clings to his wife,
and the two become one flesh.

—Genesis 2:24

Now you will feel no rain
        For each of you will be
            shelter to the other.
        Now you will feel no cold
For each of you will be warmth to the other.
Now you will feel no loneliness
For each of you will be
    companionship to the other.
Now you are two persons
But there is only one life between you.

Go now to your dwelling place
To enter into the days of your life together.

—American Indian Wedding Prayer

Holy is the taking
and the giving
of love.

—Hoyt Axton

Prayer

Love and commitment to each other,
shall not negate truth to one's own self...
for it is only by making yourself
whole that you will be able to fulfill the
commitments of a loving relationship.
Care for, and tend to, your own life needs
and problems so that you may bring to
each other your greatest strengths, your
most tender kindness, and your deepest
wisdom. For you cannot protect and heal
another until you are yourself protected
and healed ... and you cannot show soft
compassion until you are yourself in
control of all of your giving qualities ...
you will know when that time of golden
love has come ... for it is then that you
are truly wed ... at that moment when
your hearts touch and join in the
communion of the silent, unspoken bond
of marriage.

—Diane Westlake

A good marriage is one where love is not destroyed. Love changes, of course, in its manifestation as time goes on and as individuals achieve higher levels of maturity, but change does not mean destruction. It can and should mean growth. A good marriage is one which allows for change and growth in the individuals and in the way they express their love.

—Pearl S. Buck

A Marriage Covenant

I am marrying you because I want to be close to you,
    to have and to hold.
And because I want to experience all that life has to offer
    living with you.
Each of us will continue to be our own person,
    supporting the other in our learning and growth,
    adding to and never taking from what each of us can be.
I want and give you friendship as well as love.
    Let us play, create, achieve, and work together as equals.
When our individual differences are in conflict,
    let us resolve them without hurting,
    and store up not one day or night of resentment.
When either of us is hurting, or is afraid,
    let there be all the compassion we need.
Of respect for ourselves and each other, of trust and honor,
    let there be enough to fill our needs.
When to each other or another we make commitments,
    let's keep them as best we can, and make no commitments
    we don't intend to keep.
Of appreciation and acknowledgement of our deeds,
    let there be praise enough.
Let the security and happiness of each of us,
    be equally important to both of us.
Reach out, come close, and stay near, for there is a special
    pleasure in our touching.
I am a loving person and I have love to give.
    You I choose to love. I need you to love me.
    Your love I receive.
Let these words, in all their meaning, be our covenant,
    made between us this day,
    and as long as we both shall LOVE.

—Jack V. Crawford

There is no peace
  Without harmony
No harmony
  Without music

There is no music
  Without song
No song
  Without beauty

There is no beauty
  Without laughter
No laughter
  Without joy

There is no joy
  Without kindness
No kindness
  Without caring

No caring
  Without love
No love
  Without you

—Leonard Nimoy

I love you
the more in that I believe
you have liked me for my
own sake and for nothing else.

—John Keats

The most
beautiful gift
we can give
each other
is the truth.

—Anonymous

Love

There is no difficulty that enough love
will not conquer; No disease that enough
love will not heal; No door that enough love
will not open; No gulf that enough love will
not bridge; No wall that enough love will not
throw down; No sin that enough love
will not redeem . . .

It makes no difference how deeply
seated may be the trouble;
How hopeless the outlook; How muddled
the tangle; How great the mistake.
A sufficient realization of love will dissolve
it all . . . If only you could love enough you
would be the happiest and most powerful
being in the world . . .

—Emmet Fox

One must love
not sometimes only,
for a passing moment,
but always.

—Feodor Dostoevski

Grow old along with me!
  The best is yet to be,
The last of life, for which the first
    was made:
  Our times are in his hand
  Who saith "A whole I planned,
Youth shows but half; trust God:
    see all, nor be afraid!"

                    —Robert Browning

To My Dear and Loving Husband

If ever two were one, then surely we.
If ever man were loved by wife, then thee;
If ever wife was happy in a man,
Compare with me, ye women, if you can.
I prize thy love more than whole mines of gold
Or all the riches that the East doth hold.
My love is such that rivers cannot quench,
Nor ought but love from thee, give recompense.
Thy love is such I can no way repay,
The heavens reward thee manifold, I pray.
Then while we live, in love let's so persevere
That when we live no more, we may live ever.

                    —Anne Bradstreet

What greater thing
is there
for two human souls
than to feel that they
are joined for life—
to strengthen each other
in all labor,
to rest on each other
in all sorrow,
to minister
to each other
in all pain,
and to be
with each other
in silent
unspeakable memories . . .

—George Eliot

You are the object
  of my desire
You are the sun
  and the moon to me
And I believe
  in loving you . . .
You make me so happy . . .
I believe
  in loving you

—Hoyt Axton

Love does not consist
in gazing at each other,
but in looking outward
in the same direction.

—Antoine de Saint-Exupéry

Intreat me not to leave thee,
   And to return from following after thee:
For whither thou goest, I will go;
   And where thou lodgest, I will lodge;
Thy people shall be my people,
   And thy God my God;
Where thou diest, will I die,
   And there will I be buried:
The Lord do so to me,
And more also,
   If aught but death part thee and me.

                                    —Ruth 1:16-17

Love is a spiritual coupling
   of two souls.

                    —Ben Jonson

This love of which I speak is slow to lose patience—it looks for a way of being constructive. It is not possessive: it is neither anxious to impress nor does it cherish inflated ideas of its own importance.

Love has good manners and does not pursue selfish advantage. It is not touchy. It does not compile statistics of evil or gloat over the wickedness of other people. On the contrary, it is glad with all good men when Truth prevails.

Love knows no limit to its endurance, no end to its trust, no fading of its hope: it can outlast anything. It is, in fact, the one thing that still stands when all else has fallen.

—I Corinthians 13:1-8

Let me not to the marriage of true minds
Admit impediments. Love is not love
Which alters when it alteration finds,
Or bends with the remover to remove:
Oh no! it is an ever-fixed mark,
That looks on tempests, and is never shaken;
It is the star to every wandering bark,
Whose worth's unknown, although
                                        his height be taken.
Love's not Time's fool
            though rosy lips and cheeks
Within his bending sickle's compass come;
Love alters not with his brief hours and weeks
But bears it out even to the edge of doom.

If this be error, and upon me proved,
I never writ, nor no man ever loved.

—William Shakespeare

Your heart is my heart
    Your truth is my truth
        Your feeling is my feeling

But the real strength of our love
is that we share rather than
control each other's lives

           —Susan Polis Schutz

The best and most beautiful
things in the world
cannot be seen
or even touched.
They must be felt
with the heart.

           —Helen Keller

am the sea
and you are
a raging river

You are the sun
and I am
a crystal fountain
flowing in
the growing love
of living . . .

I am you
and you are me

—Hoyt Axton

ife has become
very dear to me,
and I am
very glad that I love.
My life and my love are one.

—Vincent Van Gogh

ook to this day
for it is life
the very life of life
In its brief course lie all
the realities and truths of existence
the joy of growth
the splendor of action
the glory of power
For yesterday is but a memory
And tomorrow is only a vision
But today well lived
makes every yesterday a memory
                              of happiness
and every tomorrow a vision of hope
Look well, therefore, to this day!

—ancient Sanskrit poem

if everything happens that can't be done
(and anything's righter
than books
could plan)
the stupidest teacher will almost guess
(with a run
skip
around we go yes)
there's nothing as something as one

one hasn't a why or because or although
(and buds know better
than books
don't grow)
one's anything old being everything new
(with a what
which
around we come who)
one's everyanything so

so world is a leaf so tree is a bough
(and birds sing sweeter
than books
tell how)
so here is away and so your is a my
(with a down
up
around again fly)
forever was never till now

now i love you and you love me
(and books are shuter
than books
can be)
and deep in the high that does nothing but fall
(with a shout
each
around we go all)
there's somebody calling who's we

we're anything brighter than even the sun
(we're everything greater
than books
might mean)
we're everyanything more than believe
(with a spin
leap
alive we're alive)
we're wonderful one times one

—e. e. cummings

To accomplish great things,
we must not only act,
but also dream,
not only plan,
but also believe.

—Anatole France

Each dawn is the
beginning of a
new life
Live life day by day
to understand
the joy that is
in your heart

—Louise Bradford Lowell

Because our relationship
is based on
honesty and
fairness,
there is no
need to test
each other.
It is so
wonderful
to find someone
who I
don't need
to play games
with
and who lives
up to everything that
I consider
important, right and
beautiful.

—Susan Polis Schutz

Marriage isn't mutual ownership.
It should be an act of trust
in each other's good sense and good intentions.
If a marriage is an expression of respect,
then it can add grace to love.

—Hugh Prather

Love does not dominate;
it cultivates.

—Johann Wolfgang von Goethe

On Marriage

Let there be spaces in your togetherness,
And let the winds of heaven dance between you.

Love one another, but make not a bond of love:
Let it rather be a moving sea between the shores of
    your souls.
Fill each other's cup but drink not from one cup.
Give one another of your bread but eat not from the
    same loaf.
Sing and dance together and be joyous, but let each
    one of you be alone,
Even as the strings of a lute are alone though they
    quiver with the same music.

Give your hearts, but not into each other's keeping.
For only the hand of Life can contain your hearts.
And stand together yet not too near together:
For the pillars of the temple stand apart,
And the oak tree and the cypress grow not in each
    other's shadow.

—Kahlil Gibran

I have come to know
and love you
like I've never known
or loved another.
Words have not been made
that could describe the feelings
we have for each other.

I would go to any lengths
to let you know at all times
that I care,
because I want you to know
that anytime you reach for me,
you'll find me there.

—Dolly Parton

One of the
important aspects
of our relationship
is that neither of us
needs to be
always right, or
always strong, or
always smart, or
always first.
We have enough confidence
in ourselves and
trust in each other
that we can
be our real selves
at all times.

—Susan Polis Schutz

I love you for what you are, but I love you yet more for what you are going to be.

I love you not so much for your realities as for your ideals. I pray for your desires that they may be great, rather than for your satisfactions, which may be so hazardously little.

A satisfied flower is one whose petals are about to fall. The most beautiful rose is one hardly more than a bud wherein the pangs and ecstasies of desire are working for larger and finer growth.

Not always shall you be what you are now.

You are going forward toward something great.
I am on the way with you and therefore I love you.

—Carl Sandburg

Thank you
    For a world
        of kindness

Thank you
    For your endless
        patience

Thank you
    For your sensitive
        understanding

Thank you
    For your
        Love

—Leonard Nimoy

Personalizing your ceremony

Personalizing Your Wedding

Personalizing your wedding doesn't necessarily imply departing from traditions and having a sunrise service on a mountain peak. To give your wedding an individual touch, you should have the freedom to do as little or as much as you like. There are many alternatives to keep in mind, and the possibilities of personalizing your wedding service are nearly limitless.

Tailoring your ceremony to fit your needs is an extremely rewarding task, and one that can be as simple or as difficult as you choose to make it.

Decisions have to be made in any case — whether you choose a traditional, individual or civil ceremony. Be certain to carefully weigh all the possibilities before you finalize your wedding plans. Here is a partial list of things to be considered:

- When do we want to get married? What time of year? What time of day?
- Do we want to take an active role in writing any or all of our ceremony? If so, what words most convey our feelings for the commitment we are about to make?
- What poems, readings and musical selections should be included in the service, and how should they be performed?
- Where should the wedding take place?
- Have we considered the selection of a minister, rabbi, priest or justice who will perform the ceremony?
- How many guests, and who shall they be?
- What about invitations and programs?
- Will dress be formal or informal?
- What colors, flowers and symbols should be chosen to accent the celebration?

The list goes on and on. And yet, with so many different decisions to make, so many different roads to take, it is continually surprising that a majority of weddings seem to be molded — one after another — into patterns of similarity.

But let's consider, as we go through a list of the important elements, what changes can be made and what touches can be added to truly individualize your wedding day.

Tradition and Ceremony

The ceremony itself — the spoken words and the vows of devotion — is perhaps the most important aspect of the contemporary wedding. Too many young couples adhere to conventional vows and services simply because they are unaware of the alternatives. Although traditional vows are fostered within the church, it is interesting to note that states, rather than churches or religions, dictate the only legal requirements of a marriage.

Traditional vows can lend themselves to a beautiful ceremony, as long as relevance and rich personal meaning aren't ignored in the process.

With so many avenues to explore, where should you begin? Begin with each other, and trust your emotions, your common sense and your creativity. Request a copy of the traditional vows of your particular denominations, to be read and studied carefully. Question words and phrases you don't completely comprehend. And think about revising or deleting any wording that you find disagreeable.

Traditional wordings and customs do not fully allow for changes in societal values. Frequently requested revisions include changing "I now pronounce you man and wife" to "husband and wife," and "love, honor and obey" to simply read "love and honor." Another change is a realistic reflection of today's skyrocketing divorce rate; changing "till death do us part" or "as long as we both shall live" to a contemporary phrasing — "as long as we both shall love." Certain denominations "gather together in the fear of God." Certainly the "love of God" is a more suitable sentiment for a wedding union.

Considering Your Options

After completely studying the traditional service, the time comes to honestly and openly consider your options. Do the two of you want to work within the confines of the traditional vows, or do you want to start anew, writing your own vows and creating your own ceremony?

If you decide to alter any or all of the traditional service, discuss the matter with the person performing the ceremony. Because of the wide range of church ethics, you'll want to insure that the alteration fits in with his or her own religious confines. In the event that an interfaith marriage will be performed, be sure to speak with representatives of each denomination, and proceed with careful wording in the revised service. It should be noted though, that an interfaith marriage is quite easily adapted into a non-traditional wedding. Original writings can often bridge any gap between the two services, and creative touches can dispel any confusion between differing traditional customs.

Concepts and Creativity

After the groundwork is done — you've examined and, if necessary, revised or rejected the traditional vows, and you've confirmed that the person officiating at the wedding will be compatible with your alterations — you're ready to begin the compilation of a rough draft. This draft should be thought of as a preliminary version of what will eventually become your own special service.

Not long after you take pen in hand, you will begin to recognize that writing your own vows can be one of the most rewarding moments of the entire wedding experience. Your task is that of capturing — on paper — thoughts of your love for each other, feelings of your emotional and spiritual commitment, reflections of the roles that family and friends have played in your lives, and plans and promises the two of you have for the future.

The varied stages of creating your ceremony can be emotionally rich and educational times. The period is exemplified by sharing and compromise, characteristic of the marriage union itself.

Writing the Rough Draft

Your attention should be directed to differing stages of the wedding service. Treat the stages on an individual basis, but keep them in perspective to the entire ceremony. Especially consider the opening greeting, a wedding pledge, a wedding prayer or meditation, the marriage vows, the exchange and blessing of the rings, the marriage pronouncement and the closing words. In all aspects of revision and original writing, strive for sincerity and simplicity.

As you begin to write and insert portions into your service, you'll be continually confronted with your innermost thoughts . . . separately and together. You'll have to define and examine values oriented toward the individual and the relationship. You'll discover things about each other you never even realized before. You'll know the joy of discovering words and phrases within yourselves that will perfectly express — to each other and to all who attend — the completeness of your feelings and beliefs. And above all else, you'll have the opportunity of working — two together — toward a beautiful and ceremonious goal.

When writing your own vows, the only bounds you're subject to are the limits of your imagination. Think in terms of the whole — the entire ceremony — and the effect you wish to achieve. Keep the tone of the wedding in mind: are you trying to reflect a solemn or a joyous occasion? The formality of your spoken service will act as the basis for either choice.

Length is an important consideration. A long, drawn-out ceremony is justifiable only in rare circumstances. Try to avoid any obscure references or confusing symbolic passages in the ceremony. Anything less than obvious may require an explanation, either in the program or in the service itself. And remember that your written words are to be spoken (and heard) in the ceremony. With this in mind, read your rough draft aloud and, if possible, make a tape recording of the spoken service. Revise any passages that aren't easily enunciated and consider editing any selections that are difficult to read because of length or placement. Try to maintain transitions between the various sections of your ceremony, and follow a logical progression through beginning, middle and end.

Selecting Poems and Prose Readings

Poems and prose readings can provide a flowing and lyrical touch to any wedding, be it civil, traditional or contemporary. When compiling the format of a service, think of the moments in your ceremony that are most appropriate for a poetic interjection. Once again, the choices are entirely yours.

Some couples prefer that a poetic selection about love or marriage be included in the opening welcome. Other couples might select a particular passage to be read in accordance with the marriage vows. And many couples include a poem meant to capture the mood of their ceremony following the exchange of rings and preceeding their exit from the altar.

Whatever your reasons, whatever your placement of poems and prose excerpts in the service, make your own personal selections and have fun doing it. Remembering "old stand-bys" and discovering new-found favorites is nothing short of an adventure.

A number of wedding favorites are included in the first chapter of this book. But if you're in need of a mood or a sentiment that has been overlooked, there are infinite varieties of poems and writings to perfectly express your emotions. Perhaps you could quote something from the person you most admire in life. Or if the spirit moves you, you might want to author or co-author your own wedding poems or lyrics. Look to yourselves for inspiration, and try to define the sentiment you want to express.

Go through old love letters and diary entries to recall a special moment or a certain phrase that seems to verbalize the essence of your feelings for each other. Or if you have a difficult time writing an original poem, you may choose to take a favorite piece and interpret or paraphrase it.

Try to recall Bible passages that have special significance. Ask the person performing the ceremony to suggest verses that adapt themselves to benedictions and wedding prayers.

Browse through shops and libraries, confer with friends and family, and read through the selections in this book to find the perfect reflections of your marriage, your life-style and your commitment. You'll find the search to be a beautiful experience . . . one that will ultimately redefine and reinforce your love for one another.

Music and the Occasion

If you've ever doubted that music is the universal language, make a point of attending a wedding where the music is carefully selected and performed to accent the mood of the entire service. Selecting music to be played at your wedding is probably the easiest decision you will be confronted with.

You might already have a number of favorite styles and titles in mind, and it is even likely that the two of you have a certain song that you've come to identify with. The only basic rule to keep in mind is that the songs should be compatible with the tone of the occasion.

Joyous songs like Bach's "Jesu, Joy of Man's Desiring" can evoke feelings of unity and encourage smiles of delight at even the most solemn wedding. Paul Williams' "We've Only Just Begun" is a contemporary favorite, for it, like Paul Stookey's "The Wedding Song", flavors a wedding with beautiful lyrics, appropriate music and the opportunity to be performed in a variety of styles.

Be certain to consider your resources in musical selection. If you are musically inclined and familiar with a suitable instrument (guitar and piano are particularly appropriate), you should think of adding your own talents to the repertoire. Otherwise, evaluate your possibilities for instrumental and vocal performers, and limit your musical selections accordingly. A very distinctive touch can be added to the musical segment of a wedding by including yourselves in the vocal performance. Granted, a little courage helps out at a moment like this, but practice and familiarity make way for confidence.

Including Your Guests

A number of beautiful and emotional experiences can occur at a wedding...events that include guest participation. Sing-alongs and read-alongs are obvious examples. But silence is equally as effective, as with the planned moment for a silent group prayer. You might also choose to reserve a moment in your ceremony to act as a vehicle for all present who are married to reaffirm their own vows.

Symbols can play an important role in guest involvement: flowers, candles, rings — practically whatever the occasion demands and your heart desires. A very lovely bridal bouquet is a work of art, and a great deal of thought and effort can be put into its selection. But the bridal bouquet could be even more beautiful — in spirit and in sentiment — if composed in a guest-related manner. This can be achieved by having an attendant greet each guest at the door with a flower and a small note or explanation. It should be requested that the gift of each flower be given to the bride, either during or following the ceremony. The giving of individual flowers allows the opportunity for an exquisite time of sharing and symbolic love. The touching end result is that of an entire bouquet, completely assembled from the wishes and blessings of everyone you've chosen to share in your wedding day.

Guest participation can be encouraged with candles, kisses, balloons or bells . . . whatever your two imaginations can invent. Simply review the possibilities, and be practical in their application. A very expressive means of guest involvement — if practically applied — entails the formation of a circle, either with or around the couple to be married. This element could be added to various portions of the ceremony, but is particularly appropriate for the blessing of the rings. With everyone present holding hands, male and female, family and friends, a common bond is formed and felt by all. The encircling energy is not unlike that of the wedding ring itself, having no beginning and no end, and existing as a token of love and an expression of unity, embracing life as a whole.

When writing your ceremony, include brief descriptions of community interaction in the rough draft.

Composing the Final Draft

With the exception of anything that may happen spontaneously, all steps, stages and spoken words should be set down on paper. With your rough draft in hand, go over your ceremony, reviewing your plans and vows from beginning to end. Read through and walk through a sample service, imagining pauses for prayer, singing songs, reciting poetry and pronouncing vows.

Then ask yourselves: Does the service accomplish the difficult task of meeting your requirements? Does it capture the perfect mood? Does it express your philosophies and feelings of marriage? And does it reflect your own personalities with sincerity?

If the final effect is natural rather than forced, and personal without being obscure, you've just completed the text and testimony of your commitment to each other.

When transposing your ceremony from rough draft to final version, be sure to highlight individual moments in the service, names of speakers, times for musical accompaniment and anything else that requires definition.

Copies of this final draft will then be used as guidelines for rehearsal and for the wedding itself. You'll probably want to enclose the pages in some type of binding, both for utilization and appearance' sake.

Programs and Invitations

The more personalized your wedding is, the more appropriate the wedding program becomes. Your guests will want to share in the special atmosphere you've created, and a program will allow them the comfort of knowing the guidelines of your unique service.

It's important to include longer readings and events within the program, and mandatory to have lyrics or poems included for sing-alongs and group readings. If you are going to ask for direct guest involvement in the ceremony, add a brief note of explanation and denote the proper time of participation. A well prepared program will help an out-of-the-ordinary wedding run smoothly, and it will serve as a pleasant remembrance to all who attend.

When designing invitations to your wedding, try to duplicate the personal touch you've achieved in your wedding service. Feature a special poem on your invitations, and if you have especially nice penmanship, talk with a local printer about reproducing your handwriting onto all your invitations. Directions and diagrams to the wedding and reception may also be necessary to include with invitations, especially when out-of-town guests will be arriving.

Settings and Symbols

After combining your imagination with your geographic location, you'll soon realize that there are many possible settings to choose from. A church or synagogue might be perfectly suited to your needs. Or you might explore the possibilities of getting married in your family's home, in a friend's garden, a nearby park, a restaurant, a wildlife sanctuary or even a planetarium. Your favorite place — maybe a secluded beach or a mountain meadow — could be the perfect setting for your ceremony. Whatever the location, just be sure that it is compatible with the tone and atmosphere of your service. Keep accessibility and practicality in mind.

Your use of symbols, colors and "props" in the ceremony can help you work toward a unified atmosphere. Beyond the tradition that the bride should have "something old, something new, something borrowed and something blue," you'll both have to make decisions about color and style of dress, wedding rings, flowers and a variety of wedding-related items. Do you want bells to ring in joyous celebration, or would you prefer that candles serve to heighten the solemnity of the occasion? Whatever you choose with regard to special elements in the service, try to conform with the spirit and the individuality of the ceremony as a whole.

The Task Set Before You

It's true. The two of you have many decisions to be made with regard to giving your wedding a personal touch. But you've already made the most important decision of all . . . that of offering to share your lives and your love with each other in a truly holy communion.

Making your wedding day a reflection of your personalities can only help to express that communion to all who attend — family and friends — who will recognize and sanctify your first precious moments as husband and wife.

Best wishes for a beautiful wedding and a happy life . . . together.

Douglas Pagels

A personal wedding

A Sample Service

After everyone is seated, the processional begins.

Song: "Morning Has Broken" (instrumental)

Officiant: We come together in a spirit
    of reverence and love
to celebrate a truly joyous occasion.
Today is a day of harmony and unison,
a day when songs and sermons sing
    of new paths to follow.
Today is a moment of trust and of faith,
a moment when poems and prayers speak
    of new bridges to build.
Today is a time of hope and new horizons,
a time when we witness beauty in giving,
    and bounty in giving endlessly.
For today we gather to join in
    matrimony _____ and _____ .

Groom (to all present): Your presence here represents a wealth beyond words. As our parents, our family and our dearest friends, much of the fabric of our lives has been woven by your hands.

Bride (to all present): You have added richness, support and meaning to our lives. As our teachers, confidants and companions, you have taught us that reciprocal love is the most wonderful of all things in life. We have tried to learn the lesson well. Thank you for sharing in a day that you — yourselves — have helped to make possible.

(Bride and groom give a rose to each other's mother while officiant recites . . .)

Officiant:
"Look to this day
for it is life
the very life of life
In its brief course lie all
the realities and truths of existence
the joy of growth
the splendor of action
the glory of power
For yesterday is but a memory
And tomorrow is only a vision
But today well lived
makes every yesterday
        a memory of happiness
and every tomorrow a vision of hope
Look well, therefore, to this day!"

Officiant: _____ and _____ , the vows which you are about to make are as sacred as any that can be made. They serve as an affirmation of mutual love, natural unity and life itself.

It has been said that "two people who love each other are in a place more holy than the interior of a church." As we speak in this garden today, how readily that notion becomes apparent. Everywhere around us, natural processes are taking place. The most precious elements of God's world combine with such ease that we too seldom acknowledge them for being the miracles that they really are.

Beginnings are to be cherished. From the seeds of a relationship can come the flowers and fruits of joy and sanctuary. A good marriage demands growth and requires care and continual attention, but it can be harvested at will, and its favorite season is always the one it is in.

Thanks be to love and a willingness to work with the elements, marriage is one of the quiet miracles of our world.

Officiant (to bride): _____ , will you have _____ to be your wedded husband? Will you love him, comfort him, honor and keep him in sickness and in health; will you share with him your fears and your failures, your aspirations and triumphs, your hopes and dreams from this day forward?

Bride: I will.

Officiant (to groom): _____ , will you have _____ to be your wedded wife? Will you love her, comfort her, honor and keep her in sickness and in health; will you share with her your fears and your failures, your aspirations and triumphs, your hopes and dreams from this day forward?

Groom: I will.

Song: "Since You've Asked" (guitar and vocals)

Groom (to bride): _____ , I pledge myself to you, to be your husband. It is my vow to love you and stay by you, furnishing smiles and support, giving challenge and encouraging growth, understanding our individuality and cherishing our oneness. You are my beloved and you are my friend.

Bride (to groom): _____ , I pledge myself to you, to be your wife. It is my vow to create for us a love that grows deeper with each passing day in honesty, faith and tenderness; a love that will enrich our lives separately and together; a love that respects our uniqueness and celebrates our union. You are my beloved and you are my friend.

Officiant: May I ask everyone present to come forward and join hands in a circle around _____ and _____ .

As Emerson said, "The eye is the first circle, the horizon which it forms is the second; and throughout nature this primary figure is repeated without end. It is the highest emblem in the cipher of the world."

The act of giving and receiving rings reminds us that love itself is an act of giving and receiving the most that life has to offer. These golden circles are the natural symbols for enduring love. They represent an inward belief and trust in togetherness. They represent an outward sign of spirit and commitment, signifying to all the bond of marriage the two of you share.

Bride (to groom): _____ , I offer this ring as a token of my love. With this ring, I thee wed, in the warmth and witness of all present.

Groom (to bride): _____ , I offer this ring as a token of my love. With this ring, I thee wed, in the warmth and witness of all present.

Bride, groom and officiant join circle of friends, and all hold hands.

Officiant: Quietly we pause in the joyful mystery that is taking place. Hearts are full. Happiness is with us now. Hopes are directed to Heaven and to earth.

A new life is beginning. Expectantly we pause and turn to Thee. Bless this marriage and let love be ever present. In the name of all that is eternal. Amen.

*At this point, the best man and maid of honor proceed to the side of the circle, directly opposite the bride and groom. They light two of the candles which were given to everyone before the service.

As the best man and maid of honor return to their places, the flame is passed from person to person, candle to candle, in each direction of the circle. Eventually, the flame of the candles will reach the bride on one side and the groom on the other. When the entire circle is complete with candles burning, all pause for a brief moment of silent prayer.

Officiant: Let us take a moment to pray, to meditate, to give _____ and _____ all our hopes and energies, all our loves and wishes that they so deeply deserve.

*After a short pause, the bride and groom depart to the center of the circle, candles in hand, to light a single large candle from the flame of the candles they hold.

They then return to the circle of friends, and blow out the candles they hold in their hands. Everyone else follows their suggestion. One candle, burning brightly, remains.

Officiant: From many lights, both past and present, two lights are formed.
From two lives, a home is born.

Groom: Each anniversary we will light this candle in memory of this day of joy.

Bride: It will remind us both of our love mutually pledged and of the light and warmth of all present today.

Officiant: May you celebrate the love you share, today and always, in ever widening circles of joy.

We now pronounce you husband and wife.

(the couple embraces . . .)

Final song: Bach's "Jesu, Joy of Man's Desiring" (guitar instrumental)

With open-minded understanding
    between us,
let's both feel free to talk . . .
In our love
    let's share a friendship between us
always close enough to talk things out

Let's be honest with ourselves
    and with each other . . .
An honest love
    is love that will survive

—Dolly Parton